The Ultimate Guide to Planning Your Personal Finances - Mike
Bernstein

ISBN: 978-1-7353939-2-6

Disclaimer

The material in this publication is of the nature of general comment only, and does not represent professional advice. It is not intended to provide specific guidance for particular circumstances and it should not be relied on as the basis for any decision to take action or not take action on any matter which it covers.

Readers should obtain professional advice where appropriate, before making any such decision. To the maximum extent permitted by law, the author and publisher disclaim all responsibility and liability to any person, arising directly or indirectly from any person taking or not taking action based on the information in this publication.

The Ultimate Guide to Planning Your Personal Finances

Mike Bernstein

Table of Contents

Preface

It looks like a big mountain in front of me! How am I going to climb it? How about one step at a time?

At 36 years old, I was watching a sporting event on TV, marveling at the participants' skills, not just at how fast they were at the event, but that they could cut through the hours of exercise and push through to the finish. It was an Ironman Triathlon (2.4-mile swim, 112-mile bike, and a 26.2-mile marathon run). I said to myself—I can't swim 2.4 miles in the ocean, no way!

I have been a long-distance runner since I was 8 years old. I had completed many races over the 28 years including several marathons, but I was not really a swimmer, or a biker. Yes, I can swim a bit (incorrectly) and I can ride a bike, but that is not the same as doing it efficiently, and for a long time. I was very fearful of a long swim, and I did not have the right type of bike.

First, I had to make the decision that I was going to cross that Ironman Triathlon finish line someday in the near future (say 2-4 years). I did that – I made the decision. I did not know exactly how I was going to get to that point, but my mind was made up.

As I continued my running, I used my off-road bicycle (big tires) to train a bit. I then convinced a friend to join me in participating in a short triathlon . . . let's see how this works out. It was a triathlon in Imperial Beach, CA. I had a spring wetsuit for wakeboarding, had the off-road bike, and I knew the run was going to be fine (1000-meter swim, 20-mile bike and 6.2-mile run). That swim (in the ocean) was my first lesson about not quite being ready. Not being able to swim with my head down (the proper way) caused me to take a very long time to finish the swim, and it was not a pretty picture (regular stroke, sidestroke, dog paddle, whatever got me through). I gathered myself after the swim, got on the bike, and put the swim behind me. Using an off-road bike for this portion of the race made it harder than it should have been, and caused a bit of embarrassment as everyone else had a road bike (skinny tires . . . rolls a lot easier). Another lesson learned. Along came the run, and I was able to excel at this leg of the race. I finished the short distance triathlon feeling schooled, but proud. The feeling of crossing the finish line was exactly what I was hoping for—the feeling of completing a worthwhile journey.

I was ready to move forward on my training to participate in triathlons with longer distances. I immediately enrolled in swimming lessons, purchased a proper wetsuit, purchased a proper road bike, and off I went. Practice, practice, practice. Within about 6 months, I decided to enter a Half Ironman. Let's use the skills I had been practicing. As with the first triathlon, I chewed off a bit more than I was ready for. But now, I could swim with better efficiency (although still learning), and the biking distance (56 miles) was hard, but I suffered through. And as usual, my running was better than most, but I was coming from behind due to my beginner swim and bike skills. The big win here was that I was not embarrassed. Although beat up a bit, I had successfully completed a Half Ironman, and yes, that feeling of accomplishment was waiting for me at the finish line.

Fast forward approximately one year later, there I am, in Panama City, Florida, standing on the beach at 7 a.m. with my trusted friend, ready to run into the ocean to start an Ironman Triathlon! When the horn sounded, my friend and I ran in the water with the other 1,700 participants, fighting the waves to get out to open water. Each leg of the Ironman was a journey in itself, and it took a lot of concentration to keep my attention on each leg, rather than on the whole race. Approximately 15 hours later, at about 10 p.m., I crossed the finish line. Okay, so the winner did it in about 8.5 hours, but who cares; I had met my goal – to finish! The feeling of accomplishment was overwhelming and fantastic. I had done what I saw on TV two years earlier (So much for "I could never swim 2.4 miles." . . . **Never Say You Can't**).

The training and completion of the Ironman allowed me to have the confidence to take on several other events that I once thought I had no chance of completing. Some of these events/sports included a 12-hour run in Texas, a 100-mile run in Arkansas, CrossFit Insanity training, and Spartan Beast.

Just as I have utilized training techniques I learned earlier in my sports life to accomplish more difficult goals, you can apply the same techniques to other tasks in your life.

You may say that there is no comparison of an Ironman Triathlon to performing proper financial and life planning for your family. I

disagree. Like any task involved in life, you must first decide you are going to do it. Then take it a step at a time. Do not think at first about the entire journey, rather concentrate on each piece at a time. Maybe the Big 6 should really be the Big 7; I should add a sporting event to the list!

The Big 6 of Stable Personal Finance

When Andres and Gina first came to Bernstein Financial Services 25 years ago, their goal was to prepare a financial plan. They realized the importance of having a professional taking care of their finances. However, they didn't know that taxes were only one piece of the financial management puzzle.

After discussing the situation, Andres and Gina started to understand the significance of financial planning. The newlywed couple was still in the early stages of life, and they wanted a worry-free and secure future.

The first thing that they decided to focus on was retirement planning. This was a good idea, as everyone should start preparing for retirement early. The last thing you want is to get near retirement age and realize that your finances are out of order. If this happens, you won't be able to enjoy your golden years as much as you should.

Next, we helped them sort out their insurance. Our experts helped them consider all the situations in which insurance can be of utmost importance. With this in mind, Andres and Gina got all the types of insurance that they needed, many of which are still in place.

Fast forward a couple of years and Andres and Gina had a child. And then another. With these exciting additions to their family came the need to extend their life insurance. We helped them ensure that their life insurance covered their kids, putting their minds at ease.

At this point, we started working on estate planning, which would protect Andres and Gina's entire family. At the same time, we continued to work on the retirement plan, tax planning, cash flow, and other relevant aspects of their financial health.

But there was another aspect that we needed to address – college planning. They wanted to ensure that, by the time their kids went to college, they wouldn't have to worry about whether they could afford it or not.

And this is exactly what happened. Thanks to careful planning, Andres and Gina could send their kids to college without any burden or worries.

Today, their kids are grown-up. Unlike many families, they managed to raise their kids without financial troubles. But this isn't because they're richer than most; it's because they prepared on time. What's more, we're still working with Andres and Gina to help manage their finances wisely, ensuring peace of mind and stability.

The Value of Planning

We're proud to say that Andres and Gina are clients who've gone through an ideal life scenario from the aspect of financial planning. Sadly, many people aren't in the same position. They don't think enough about the future, which brings about a wealth of trouble.

Some of them think that they're planning for the future just because they've bought life insurance. But what they're really doing is going about their financial planning and management randomly.

To truly plan your finances wisely, you need all of the things that Andres and Gina covered. And by the time you finish this book, you'll know exactly what it takes to create a secure and stable financial future.

Many people have anxiety, guilt and shame associated with finances. You are reminded of this as you nervously wait to meet with your tax/financial professional to go over your planning. Perhaps you have made some poor financial choices and now have some regrets. A seasoned advisor will treat you with respect and not make you feel bad about the past choices, rather support your willingness to be present and do planning forward .....
learn the facts, the options, have them laid out in front of you.

The Big 6!

1. **Cash Flow Planning**

2. **Insurance Planning**

3. **Retirement Planning**

4. **College Planning**

5. **Estate Planning**

6. **Tax Planning**

CHAPTER ONE

This Is Where It Starts: The Framework for Efficient Cash Flow Planning

When Mr. Belton wanted to retire, his wife didn't think that this would be possible. She came to Bernstein Financial for help as she didn't think her husband could afford retirement. Like most people, Mrs. Belton just made an assumption as she hadn't done the actual numbers.

To get a clear picture of her household's financials, Mrs. Belton agreed to make a cash flow plan. We helped her create one and, to her surprise, found out there was enough money for Mr. Belton to retire.

However, there was a problem – Mrs. Belton wasn't sure if she wanted her husband at home all the time. Now, this was a big part of the issue, not just the money.

Bernstein Financial helped Mr. and Mrs. Belton sort out their retirement plan and encouraged them to discuss all the issues surrounding retirement. We covered all the important aspects and managed to get the couple on the same page. Mr. Belton happily retired, and the couple is now satisfied with their lifestyle.

This story highlights an important issue that many people face. They do not do any cash flow planning because they're afraid. Like Mrs. Belton, many are scared of looking at their lifestyle in greater detail. They don't want to face reality and see how much money they're spending. If this is you, don't worry, it is quite normal, but if left unattended, it can be very dangerous.

It's vital to take a close look at your finances and be honest with your spending. If you don't, it's impossible to do any kind of financial planning.

If you're not sure where to start, the following sections will give you the guidance that you need.

What to Do if You Want to Save for Retirement but Can't Do It

Why are you not able to save for retirement?

If you're like most people, the reason will be clear enough – you can't afford to.

But the reality is, a lack of money is almost never a problem; a lack of planning is. And this is why cash flow planning is the backbone of financial management.

The thing is, many people think of cash flow planning as budgeting. They see it as something restrictive and limiting. People believe that they'll have to sacrifice many things that they love spending money on. After all, nobody likes hearing that they're overindulging on clothes, entertainment, and other things.

If this is how you see cash flow planning, you need to change your mindset as soon as possible. It's not about budgeting or stripping your life down to the basics. Rather, it's about forecasting and using your money in a smart way.

Without cash flow planning, you won't be able to plan for retirement. You also won't be able to do any insurance planning, college planning, or any other vital form of financial forecasting.

If you're not planning your cash flow, you don't have a grip on the future. Instead, you're living paycheck-to-paycheck, trying to find the best way to spread your budget throughout the month.

Obviously, this isn't the best way to go about your finances. What you should do is predict the future instead of leaving it to chance, but baring your spending habits is not easy. So go to a planner who will not make you feel bad!

As one client told me after we did some planning.....

"So we shared our situation, and waited for a response. What, No Judgment? Mike reaffirmed that the important thing was to take an honest look at where we were at and where we would like to be. 'Coming clean' regarding over-spending, credit card debt can be embarrassing. Once we did, however, given the proper guidance and support, IT FELT LIKE A RELIEF. We shared our concerns, and found out that many others have gone through similar experiences. We were not alone in our world of financial anxiety. What next?"

Are You Cash Flow Positive? – Roll up Your Sleeves and Do the Excel Planning Spreadsheet

Cash flow planning is as simple as putting the numbers down on a piece of paper. A standard Excel sheet will do, or you can go old-school with a pen and paper. It doesn't matter how you do it, as long as you can get a clear overview of your monthly inflow and outflow.

No matter if you're single or married, with or without kids, the process is the same. Your goal here is to compare your household income and expenses side by side.

Start by listing your net pay coming in. You already have the taxes figured out and set aside, so write down your monthly disposable income. If you have bonuses, put them in the months when they happen. And if they vary throughout the year, add them up and divide by 12 to get a monthly average.

Now, that was the easy part. The hard part is to list all your expenses, as they can vary more from month to month.

Start by writing down the fixed expenses like your mortgage or rent. If the mortgage doesn't include the property tax that you pay twice a year, add it up and divide by 12. Remember that everything should be monthly, even if that's not how you're paying for it.

Aside from the mortgage/rent, put down your car lease if you have one. If there are any repairs that you need to do, make sure to include them as well. Look at your history and make a yearly estimate, which you'll then divide by 12.

If you go on vacations, draw an average of how much you spend on them per year. Do the same for non-travel entertainment such as dining out, movies, and so on. Of course, you should also make this monthly.

Next, include your groceries, as well as all expenses related to your kids. This includes everything from clothes and schooling to parties and gifts.

There are many other expenses that you should include, but you get the idea. Leave no stone unturned, and make sure that you're honest with the numbers. Once you do, you'll be able to see if you're cash flow positive or negative.

So, what happens then?

Sample
John and Sally Jones (ages 34 and 33)
Child 5 years old

Projection : 1/1/20XX - 12/31/20XX

Revenue Net (net W2 wages)

	January	February	March	April	May	June	July	August	September	October	November	December	Year
John	$5,000	$5,000	$5,000	$5,000	$5,000	$5,000	$5,000	$5,000	$5,000	$5,000	$5,000	$5,000	$60,000
John bonus				$5,000									$5,000
Sally	$2,000	$2,000	$2,000	$2,000	$2,000	$2,000	$2,000	$2,000	$2,000	$2,000	$2,000	$2,000	$24,000
Total Revenue	$7,000	$7,000	$7,000	$12,000	$7,000	$7,000	$7,000	$7,000	$7,000	$7,000	$7,000	$7,000	$89,000

Expenses

	January	February	March	April	May	June	July	August	September	October	November	December	Year
Mortgage, taxes and home Ins	$1,870	$1,870	$1,870	$1,870	$1,870	$1,870	$1,870	$1,870	$1,870	$1,870	$1,870	$1,870	$22,440
Life Insurance	$125	$125	$125	$125	$125	$125	$125	$125	$125	$125	$125	$125	$1,500
Gardening	$75	$75	$75	$75	$75	$75	$75	$75	$75	$75	$75	$75	$900
Time Warner	$50	$50	$50	$50	$50	$50	$50	$50	$50	$50	$50	$50	$600
Telephone	$150	$150	$150	$150	$150	$150	$150	$150	$150	$150	$150	$150	$1,800
Utilities	$75	$75	$75	$75	$75	$75	$75	$75	$75	$75	$75	$75	$900
Vehicle exp	$200	$200	$200	$200	$200	$200	$200	$200	$200	$200	$200	$200	$2,400
Vehicle payment	$350	$350	$350	$350	$350	$350	$350	$350	$350	$350	$350	$350	$4,200
Cash/Miscellaneous	$600	$600	$600	$600	$600	$600	$600	$600	$600	$600	$600	$600	$7,200
Medical	$300	$300	$300	$300	$300	$300	$300	$300	$300	$300	$300	$300	$3,600
Groceries	$800	$800	$800	$800	$800	$800	$800	$800	$800	$800	$800	$800	$9,600
Newspaper	$50	$50	$50	$50	$50	$50	$50	$50	$50	$50	$50	$50	$600
Vacations	$250	$250	$250	$250	$250	$250	$250	$250	$250	$250	$250	$250	$3,000
sports conditioning	$100	$100	$100	$100	$100	$100	$100	$100	$100	$100	$100	$100	$1,200
Entertainment/eating out	$200	$200	$200	$200	$200	$200	$200	$200	$200	$200	$200	$200	$2,400
Child Care Expenses/school	$500	$500	$500	$500	$500	$500	$500	$500	$500	$500	$500	$500	$6,000
After Tax investment	$250	$250	$250	$250	$250	$250	$250	$250	$250	$250	$250	$250	$3,000
College savings	$200	$200	$200	$200	$200	$200	$200	$200	$200	$200	$200	$200	$2,400
Credit Card Debt paydown	$200	$200	$200	$200	$200	$200	$200	$200	$200	$200	$200	$200	$2,400
total expenses	$6,345	$6,345	$6,345	$6,345	$6,345	$6,345	$6,345	$6,345	$6,345	$6,345	$6,345	$6,345	$76,140
Balance left	$655	$655	$655	$5,655	$655	$655	$655	$655	$655	$655	$655	$655	$12,860
Balance left - YTD	$655	$1,310	$1,965	$7,620	$8,275	$8,930	$9,585	$10,240	$10,895	$11,560	$12,205	$12,860	

Net Worth (assets less liabilities)

	12/31/XX	Plus 1 years	Plus 2 years	Plus 3 years	Plus 4 years	Plus 5 years
Checking	$1,200	$1,200	$1,800	$2,000	$2,250	$2,500
Savings	$7,000	$8,000	$10,000	$12,000	$14,000	$10,000
401K John	$40,000	$46,000	$53,000	$60,000	$70,000	$81,000
401K Sally	$30,000	$35,000	$40,000	$46,000	$53,000	$60,000
After tax investment account	$10,000	$13,500	$17,000	$25,000	$32,000	$40,000
House	$350,000	$360,500	$371,315	$382,454	$393,928	$405,746
College Acct	$2,500	$4,900	$7,500	$11,500	$17,500	$26,000
car	$20,000	$18,000	$16,000	$14,000	$10,000	$30,000
car	$12,000	$10,000	$8,000	$6,000	$5,000	$17,000
Total	**$472,700**	**$497,100**	**$524,615**	**$558,954**	**$597,678**	**$672,246**
CC 1	$3,500	$2,500	$1,400	$ -	$ -	$ -
CC 2	$4,500	$3,500	$2,500	$1,400	$ -	$ -
Home loan	$200,000	$195,000	$190,000	$185,000	$180,000	$175,000
Car loan	$13,000	$11,500	$8,750	$5,500	$2,500	$25,000
Total	**$213,000**	**$206,500**	**$198,750**	**$190,500**	**$182,500**	**$200,000**
Net Equity	**$259,700**	**$290,600**	**$325,865**	**$368,454**	**$415,178**	**$472,246**

How Do I Fix a Negative Cash Flow or Make the Positive One Even Better?

When going through the above exercise, you won't get a perfectly clear picture right away. Instead, you'll have to go back to the list a few times before you get it right. You'll forget some expenses at first, so you'll have to update the list for two or three months before you have it all laid out.

Also, keep in mind that the goal here is to get an objective overview of your cash flow and what you can do about it. Don't focus on what you wish the numbers were, but rather, be fully realistic. In addition, don't argue with your partner or family. This isn't the time to pin the blame for spending. All you have to do is see where you stand financially.

So, what happens if your cash flow is negative? What if it's positive but you need it to be more abundant?

Broadly speaking, there are two options here. The first one is to trim your expenses. Once you have a detailed overview of your outgoings, see which of them you can cut. Maybe you can spend less on entertainment, vacations, or other extras. You may have to downsize and move into a smaller house or apartment. If you haven't already, maybe you need to refinance your mortgage or credit.

The best thing that you can do is talk to a financial advisor and explore your options. In many cases, a few lifestyle changes can amount to a lot of saved money.

But what if this doesn't happen? What if you look at the list and see that there's nothing that you can give up?

That's where the second option applies. And it's a pretty straightforward one – you have to make more money.

You may have to go back to school or get some informal education to get a better job. Or maybe you can just work harder at your current one. You can look for a way to supplement your income with a side job. There are many things that you can do to grow your income and improve your cash flow.

Still, this usually isn't what happens. Instead, people see that they can manage the money that they have in a better way. And the next section will explore one of the most common options for doing so.

Restructuring Debt and Making a Monthly Savings Plan

Are you drawing on debt every month or every couple of months? If so, it's a clear sign that you need to take your cash flow more seriously. You need to understand that this is a serious issue that you should fix as quickly as possible. Admitting that you have an issue is the critical aspect of fixing it. Do not feel alone, it is a common problem, but what is not common is understanding how to fix it!

As you try to fix your cash flow, you'll stumble upon many options. And debt restructuring can be the most effective one.

So how does it work?

Let's say that you have a mortgage, credit card, and personal loan. Even if you cut your current expenses, you don't think that you'll be able to pay off the credit card and personal loan. You're losing a lot of money on interest, and there's not enough left to pay for everything and still have something left at the end of the month.

In this case, you could restructure your debt to pay down the high-interest debt and save more money each month. In this specific scenario, you could refinance your mortgage to get a cash flow injection.

In addition, you could negotiate a lower debt amount with your creditor. Bear in mind, though, that this could hurt your credit score, as it would mean that you're defaulting on the original agreement.

Restructuring your loan can be an effective way to free up some cash. But it's still not enough to ensure smart financial management. Instead, you must also make a savings plan and put that extra money to good use. Only then will you start creating a solid cash flow plan.

Why It's Critical to Revisit Your Plan Each Year

A cash flow plan isn't something that you set and forget. Rather, it should be an ongoing, evolving practice. Your financial situation will change with time, and you'll want to stay on top of those changes.

This means that you'll need to revisit your cash flow plan every year. Why?

Like every other plan, your cash flow plan should serve a specific goal. And you won't achieve that goal overnight. As a result, you'll have to revisit and tweak your plan each year to account for all the changes.

Situations change all the time. Maybe you had to foreclose on a house, or were subject to earthquake or hurricane damage. You are now overwrought with expenses. You are thinking ….. what will people think about us? Okay, get that out of your mind and put all your energy toward learning to understand and weigh the options and then make a decision. You should not be justifying your choices to anyone but the people you have financial ties/responsibilities to.

Now, it's important to note that your goal shouldn't be to spend no money and cut every expense aside from the necessary ones. As we explained, it's not about sacrificing the things that you enjoy. In fact, the very opposite is true.

Your goal could be to have enough cash to afford everything that you want to do on a monthly basis. You might want to go on certain vacations throughout the year that will require some savings. Your kids might be growing up, and you want to make sure that they'll have everything that they need.

Whatever your plan is, it's important that you write it down when planning your cash flow. Doing so will show you exactly how much money you need to achieve your goals. It will be much easier to see the changes that you need to make once you have clear goals in place.

All you have to do then is figure out the most effective way to unlock more of your net income. As soon as any change to your inflow or outflow happens, you should update your plan to factor it in. With time, being smart with your money will become much more effortless.

Net Worth Statement

There's a high chance that you've heard of the concept of net worth. You might've read an article about a millionaire with the kind of net worth that most people can only dream of. But what exactly does net worth tell you?

In a nutshell, net worth is the monetary value of all the assets that you own minus all the liabilities. In other words, it's the amount of money that you'd have if you were to sell everything that you have. Knowing your net worth is important for a couple of reasons.

First, your net worth paints a clear picture of your current financial standing. It shows how well you've managed to save and grow your income so far.

Also, your net worth determines your financial health. Positive net worth that keeps increasing is a sign of good financial health. And if your net worth keeps decreasing, it's a clear sign that you need to manage your money more wisely.

In some cases, the net worth might be negative. This often happens to people who've just graduated from college. They might have no assets or a stable income while their debt might be very high. In this context, net worth describes how much you'd still owe if you sold everything and put the cash towards debt repayment. Do not let this startle you. Early debt in order to create future wealth is acceptable.

How to Calculate Your Net Worth

As mentioned, net worth is the difference between the value of your assets and your liabilities. As such, calculating your net worth is pretty simple. The first thing that you have to do is add up all your assets such as:

- The market value of your property
- Value of your car
- Money in the bank
- The dollar value of insurance
- Business interests
- Valuable items such as jewelry, furniture, and art

Of course, everyone will have their own list. The point is to add up everything that has a monetary value. When you do, you need to subtract all your liabilities including

- Mortgage
- Car loan
- Student loan
- Credit card balance, personal loan, etc.

Essentially, this is where you list all the money that you have to repay. And when you subtract it from the value of your assets, you'll have your personal net worth.

Obviously, getting a precise amount is pretty much impossible. For this reason, people estimate their net worth instead of looking for an exact figure. It's crucial that your estimates are realistic and conservative. Inflating the value of certain assets might present a distorted picture. So, be objective, crunch the numbers, and see what your financial health looks like.

Sample
John and Sally Jones (ages 34 and 33)
Child 5 years old

Projection : 1/1/20XX - 12/31/20XX

Revenue Net (net W2 wages)	January	February	March	April	May	June	July	August	September	October	November	December	Year
John	$5,000	$5,000	$5,000	$5,000	$5,000	$5,000	$5,000	$5,000	$5,000	$5,000	$5,000	$5,000	$60,000
John bonus				$5,000									$5,000
Sally	$2,000	$2,000	$2,000	$2,000	$2,000	$2,000	$2,000	$2,000	$2,000	$2,000	$2,000	$2,000	$24,000
Total Revenue	$7,000	$7,000	$7,000	$12,000	$7,000	$7,000	$7,000	$7,000	$7,000	$7,000	$7,000	$7,000	$89,000
Expenses													
Mortgage, taxes and home Ins	$1,870	$1,870	$1,870	$1,870	$1,870	$1,870	$1,870	$1,870	$1,870	$1,870	$1,870	$1,870	$22,440
Life Insurance	$125	$125	$125	$125	$125	$125	$125	$125	$125	$125	$125	$125	$1,500
Gardening	$75	$75	$75	$75	$75	$75	$75	$75	$75	$75	$75	$75	$900
Time Warner	$50	$50	$50	$50	$50	$50	$50	$50	$50	$50	$50	$50	$600
Telephone	$150	$150	$150	$150	$150	$150	$150	$150	$150	$150	$150	$150	$1,800
Utilities	$75	$75	$75	$75	$75	$75	$75	$75	$75	$75	$75	$75	$900
Vehicle exp	$200	$200	$200	$200	$200	$200	$200	$200	$200	$200	$200	$200	$2,400
Vehicle payment	$350	$350	$350	$350	$350	$350	$350	$350	$350	$350	$350	$350	$4,200
Cash/Miscellaneous	$600	$600	$600	$600	$600	$600	$600	$600	$600	$600	$600	$600	$7,200
Medical	$300	$300	$300	$300	$300	$300	$300	$300	$300	$300	$300	$300	$3,600
Groceries	$800	$800	$800	$800	$800	$800	$800	$800	$800	$800	$800	$800	$9,600
Newspaper	$50	$50	$50	$50	$50	$50	$50	$50	$50	$50	$50	$50	$600
Vacations	$250	$250	$250	$250	$250	$250	$250	$250	$250	$250	$250	$250	$3,000
sports conditioning	$100	$100	$100	$100	$100	$100	$100	$100	$100	$100	$100	$100	$1,200
Entertainment/eating out	$200	$200	$200	$200	$200	$200	$200	$200	$200	$200	$200	$200	$2,400
Child Care Expenses/school	$500	$500	$500	$500	$500	$500	$500	$500	$500	$500	$500	$500	$6,000
After Tax investment	$250	$250	$250	$250	$250	$250	$250	$250	$250	$250	$250	$250	$3,000
College savings	$200	$200	$200	$200	$200	$200	$200	$200	$200	$200	$200	$200	$2,400
Credit Card Debt paydown	$200	$200	$200	$200	$200	$200	$200	$200	$200	$200	$200	$200	$2,400
total expenses	$6,345	$6,345	$6,345	$6,345	$6,345	$6,345	$6,345	$6,345	$6,345	$6,345	$6,345	$6,345	$76,140
Balance left	$655	$655	$655	$5,655	$655	$655	$655	$655	$655	$655	$655	$655	$12,860
Balance left - YTD	$655	$1,310	$1,965	$7,620	$8,275	$8,930	$9,585	$10,240	$10,895	$11,550	$12,205	$12,860	

Net Worth (assets less liabilities)	12/31/XX	Plus 1 year	Plus 2 years	Plus 3 years	Plus 4 years	Plus 5 years
Checking	$ 1,200	$ 1,200	$ 1,800	$ 2,000	$ 2,250	$ 2,500
Savings	$ 7,000	$ 8,000	$ 10,000	$ 12,000	$ 14,000	$ 10,000
401K John	$ 40,000	$ 46,000	$ 53,000	$ 60,000	$ 70,000	$ 81,000
401K Sally	$ 30,000	$ 35,000	$ 40,000	$ 46,000	$ 53,000	$ 60,000
After tax investment account	$ 10,000	$ 13,500	$ 17,000	$ 25,000	$ 32,000	$ 40,000
House	$ 350,000	$ 360,500	$ 371,315	$ 382,454	$ 393,928	$ 405,746
College Acct	$ 2,500	$ 4,900	$ 7,500	$ 11,500	$ 17,500	$ 26,000
car	$ 20,000	$ 18,000	$ 16,000	$ 14,000	$ 10,000	$ 30,000
car	$ 12,000	$ 10,000	$ 8,000	$ 6,000	$ 5,000	$ 17,000
Total	$ 472,700	$ 497,100	$ 524,615	$ 558,954	$ 597,678	$ 672,246
CC 1	$ 3,500	$ 2,500	$ 1,400	$ 1,400	$ -	$ -
CC 2	$ 4,500	$ 3,500	$ 2,500	$ -	$ -	$ -
Home loan	$ 200,000	$ 195,000	$ 190,000	$ 185,000	$ 180,000	$ 175,000
Car loan	$ 13,000	$ 11,500	$ 8,750	$ 5,500	$ 2,500	$ 25,000
Total	$ 213,000	$ 206,500	$ 198,750	$ 190,500	$ 182,500	$ 200,000
Net Equity	$ 259,700	$ 290,600	$ 325,865	$ 368,454	$ 415,178	$ 472,246

Analyze, Plan, and Adapt

When was the last time you took a close look at your cash flow? Have you done it at all?

If not, there's no better time to start than right now. If you want to take the future into your own hands, this is the necessary first step. It allows you to know exactly where you are and what you can do to change your position.

Remember to plan your cash flow based on facts and real numbers. Don't have a judgmental approach to your cash flow analysis. Doing so will keep you living in denial so that you don't have to face your reality.

Instead, what you should do is simply put everything that you're already doing on paper. This way, you'll have the control that you need to manage your money more wisely. And this is where you can start planning other aspects of your financial future.

CHAPTER TWO

Insurance Planning – The Thing That Keeps You Sound Asleep at Night

Insurance planning is one of those things that most people don't want to talk about. They find it boring or quite uncomfortable. After all, nobody wants to think about a scenario where something unfortunate happens to them or they die.

But however scary it may seem, it's vital that you think about insurance. Otherwise, you may live a sub-standard life when you retire. And it's usually the middle-income individuals that suffer the most. To make sure this doesn't happen, you must plan for the future and think about insurance.

Remember Mr. and Mrs. Garcia from the story you read? As mentioned, they've gone through the ideal scenario from the aspect of planning. And one of the main reasons for this is that they planned their insurance right.

When they were in their sixties, Andres and Gina realized that it was time to start thinking about insurance. They were nearing retirement, and they wanted a stable, worry-free future. Because of this, they wanted to start planning their long-term care. But they didn't think that they could afford it.

After some cash flow planning, we helped them see that this wasn't the case. Andres and Gina had enough money to set aside for long-term care. And so they did.

Fast forward 15 years, Andres got Alzheimer's. He needed proper care, so Gina decided to place him in an appropriate facility. Long-term care kicked in and covered almost 90% of the costs.

While Gina was obviously very sad about what happened, at least she didn't have to worry about the financial burden of her husband's condition. He got the proper care that he needed, and Gina didn't have to struggle.

This is only one example of how proper insurance planning can make your life much more comfortable. And in this chapter, we'll dive deeper into how you can make this happen.

Everything You Need to Know About Different Types of Insurance

Every person should think about various types of insurance such as:

- Life insurance
- Long-Term Care insurance
- Health insurance
- Umbrella insurance
- Overhead insurance
- Disability insurance

Sounds like a lot, doesn't it? Well, this is the reason why so many people hesitate to do any insurance planning. But there's a massive reason to do it anyway – protecting yourself and those around you.

Life comes with many surprises, many of which might not be positive. When these happen, you want to keep yourself and your loved ones protected from the consequences. And there's no better way to do it than with insurance. So, let's talk about this kind of insurance in greater detail.

Life Insurance

The best way to explain why life insurance is important and how it works is through a hypothetical example. Picture a couple, Ruben and Vanessa, who have two kids. What would happen if Ruben died? How would his family survive without having to suffer financially?

Again, this is a scenario that people don't like to discuss. But sadly, it happens to many of us. And this is exactly why it's important to think about it.

So, let's say that Ruben died and that Vanessa had to replace his income. How would she know how much insurance she needed?

It's simple – if Ruben's salary was $80,000, she'd take $80,000 and divide it by .05 (or multiply by 20) which is equal to the insurance payout. This would mean she would buy $1.6M face amount of life insurance. Assuming a 5% (.05) earnings rate on the life insurance proceeds invested, Vanessa will earn $80,000 per year to replace Ruben's income.

Now, you might think that this is a massive number. But it's really not. It's more than possible for an average person to buy this kind of insurance and pay for it comfortably. And, as you can see, it's easy to figure out how much you need.

The only complicated thing about insurance is facing it. If you're like most people, there's a high chance that the Ruben-and-Vanessa example made you a bit uncomfortable. You must overcome this and plan for the scenarios that might affect your well-being.

It's always a good idea to start thinking about your insurance as early in life as possible. The reason for this is that the premium will be lower. Plus, there is a much better chance you will be insurable. If you face some medical issues later in life, you can rest assured that your insurance will have you covered (as you may not qualify to buy life insurance after suffering a medical issue).

Another important thing is to get life insurance outside of your workplace. Otherwise, the insurance might get tied to your job. It won't be portable, meaning that you'll lose the insurance the moment you quit your job.

And finally, you must choose the right type of life insurance to buy. There are two main types to choose from: permanent and term insurance. Permanent insurance comes with the benefit of having a cash value in it. Think of it as a savings account within your insurance that guarantees the premium won't change.

The issue is, buying permanent life insurance can be quite expensive. In Vanessa's example, buying $1.6 million of permanent insurance would cost around $800 per month. At the same time, term insurance would cost around $200. Sometimes, permanent insurance can cost five to seven times more than a term option.

Because of this, you should always start with term insurance earlier in life. And then, as your income grows, you can buy permanent insurance that will stay with you for life.

Long-Term Care Insurance

Ruben and Gina's example showcases the value of life insurance. As you saw, the insurance can prove itself to be a very valuable decision. And if you fall under the middle-income category, long term care insurance can also be especially valuable.

How so?

If you've built up enough equity that you can afford your own care, you don't have to think about long-term care insurance. Your net worth will be enough to ensure proper care if you need it.

On the other hand, if you're a low-income individual, Medicaid/Medi-Cal will take over. So, even if you're in a bad place financially, you'll still get covered.

But, if your income is average, neither of the above options will apply. Instead, you might end up in nursing care, which will exhaust all of your assets. At one point, you might end up on Medicaid anyway. You'll have no money for inheritance or any other way to take care of your family.

This is where long-term care insurance could offer the protection that you need. On average, it can provide you with three to five years of care without any additional expenses.

Of course, this would be very valuable to your family as well. They wouldn't have to manipulate their assets or sacrifice their lifestyle to afford the care that you need. With some careful planning, you can ensure a stable future for everyone you care about.

Thus far, Bernstein Financial has worked with thousands of clients. And only a small number of them had long-term care insurance before they came to us. Others only woke up to its value after we explained it to them.

Luckily, they did so in time, as they managed to preserve their assets and protect their family.

Health Insurance

There's really not much to say about health insurance except one thing:

You must absolutely have it.

We all know that healthcare is very expensive. But did you know that it's the number one cause of personal bankruptcy? This is all the proof that you need of how vital it is to have health insurance.

There's no person in the world who won't need any kind of medical care. And the vast majority of people will have accidents that will require hospitalization, surgery, or other forms of care. Just a broken leg can cost you thousands of dollars. And let's not even talk about serious or chronic health conditions.

It's not uncommon for people to take out massive loans to cover the medical bills of their loved ones or themselves. You don't want to find yourself in this situation.

Sure, you might be able to get care through the county or other means. But you certainly won't get the best care that you need this way. Plus, this won't give you any kind of preventive care.

If you don't have health insurance through your work or somebody else, you must start looking for it right away. And if you can't afford a good insurance plan on your own, you can always go with the government plans.

Medicaid, Medicare, and many other programs will provide assistance that you need if you qualify. You can contact your state-specific program to find out if you're eligible. Do your best to comply with their requirements, and don't let yourself be without health insurance for a single day in your life.

Umbrella Insurance

Umbrella insurance can be an excellent way to protect all of your assets. It's especially important if you're a business owner. If you haven't already, you should start thinking about umbrella insurance as soon as you can.

So how does it work?

Let's say that you had insurance on your house, business, and car. In this case, you could get an umbrella policy that covers them all. If any of the individual policies gets exceeded, the umbrella policy will cover another $500k-$1M.

Better yet, umbrella insurance is very inexpensive. You can get a $500k insurance policy for about $400 per year, less than $40 per month. Of course, you might want to get more than that, depending on the scope of the insurance. But still, even a $1 million insurance policy is quite affordable.

Now, some people get worried and want to put all their rentals in an LLC. While this is a good idea, it often comes at a high cost. You'd face preparation costs, state fees, and other miscellaneous expenses.

If you want to avoid these costs, a good idea is to have an umbrella policy along with a good policy against the properties. In this case, you should have all the protection that you need (please consult an attorney before you make a final decision).

Of course, combining an umbrella policy with an LLC is the ultimate protection. But there's only so much insurance that you need, so this might be excessive.

A good example of the value of umbrella insurance is a client who recently came to Bernstein Financial. He had few properties, all of which were LLCs. And in California, you have to pay $800 per LLC.

Now, the client's properties weren't big, nor were they commercial properties. Instead, they were single-family homes. We advised the client to get rid of the LLCs and get better insurance on his rentals, along with an umbrella policy.

The client consulted his lawyer, as he should've since LLCs are largely legal matters. After the lawyer gave our client the green light, he made the changes that we suggested. As a result, now they are saving some money each year, and they don't have to worry about the extra administration.

Disability Insurance

Disability insurance is another thing that can be very useful but an insurance product most people don't have. This is especially true for those who are self-employed. Many employers offer disability insurance, so you can (and should) get it through them. And if you're self-employed, there are other ways of getting the insurance that you need. Remember, this is different from the SDI through your paycheck (for wage earners). SDI is good but is limited in amount and time of payout.

Usually, disability insurance protects you until you're ready to retire. In the US, the approximate age is 67 when you're eligible for retirement and social security. Up to that point, disability insurance can cover up to 65% of your gross income.

Bear in mind that most disability insurance benefits are not taxable if you have a benefit. As a result, this 65% represents your after-tax wage. For example, if you make $10,000 per month, you should get insurance for $6,500.

The issue with disability insurance is that it doesn't build up any cash. This is one of the main reasons why people usually don't think about it. Every month that you go without making a disability claim is practically lost money as you rent the insurance. And of course, you also have to prove the disability to obtain benefits, but having the monetary benefit if you become disabled is well worth it.

Also, there will be an elimination period (from the date you become disabled to the date benefits start) that can last for 30, 60, 90, or 120 days. It's always recommended that you go with longer elimination periods, as you want to stay covered in the long run and pay the least premium.

But what if you can't afford full disability insurance?

Well, you can always go with a partial option. You can buy a partial policy that will cover a certain amount according to what you can afford. And then, as your income grows, you can always upgrade to the full policy.

Overhead Insurance

Overhead insurance isn't something that people use very often. However, if you are self-employed, it might be a good idea to get it. It can protect you from different scenarios in which you couldn't operate and could lose a lot of money; it would cover your business overhead for 1-3 years.

The way overhead insurance works is very simple. Let's say that your business overhead was $15,000 or $20,000 per month. You can buy a policy that would pay those costs back to you for up to five years. Of course, this will happen in case your business can't operate as it should.

Now, this could be due to an earthquake, flood, or any other reason beyond your control. As long as the cause is fully justified, insurance will pay your overhead back to you.

Your Future Starts Now

As you can see, there are enough types of insurance to cover every important aspect of your life. Obviously, your health is the priority, so don't expose yourself to the risk of not having health insurance. This can result in you not getting proper care or burying yourself in decades of debt.

Disability and long-term care insurance are also vital, as they can protect both you and your family. If you haven't already, you'll want to start exploring your options right now.

And as for your assets, umbrella and overhead insurance should give you the security that you need. With a good plan in place, you can ensure that, if the future does come with any unpleasant surprises, you are properly insured.

Of course, insurance isn't the only form of personal financial planning that you should do. If you have children, the next chapter will cover another aspect that you must consider.

CHAPTER THREE

Taking Care of Your Children – The Dos and Don'ts of College Planning

When Jeff and Mariam first came to Bernstein Financial, they did so because they'd made a common mistake – they didn't plan for their children's education.

The couple told our experts that they hadn't put away any money for their children's college. And the kids were already 16 and 17 years old. Because of this, they had very few options. Their plan was for the children to go to a two-year junior college, after which they'd hopefully go to a four-year college. By that time, Jeff and Mariam would explore their loan options and help children apply for grants and scholarships.

Now, this is obviously an example of how you shouldn't approach college planning. Instead, you need to start much sooner.

The thing is, not planning for college doesn't mean that your children won't actually go. Parents who want it bad enough for their children will find a way to make it work. And children who want it bad enough will work hard to do it.

But the issue is, not planning for college makes things much more complicated. You might end up like Jeff and Mariam, who now have to struggle to get their kids through college. They'll likely have to sacrifice their lifestyle in order to take out loans and help their children.

Plus, leaving children without a plan for education puts a lot of pressure on them. Some parents do this deliberately to teach their children the value of hard work and planning. And there's nothing wrong with this.

However, it may lead to your children not getting into the college they want or not being able to afford their preferred major. Also, the kids might have to go to a college in a town they don't like.

It would obviously be ideal if you could set aside $300k at once to stop this from happening. But for most parents, this isn't possible. For this reason, they need to plan their kids' education early. You must understand the compound effect and how putting away a couple of hundred dollars per month can make a world of difference. If you start early, you can make sure that college won't be a burden for you or your children.

So, have you ever thought about college planning? If not, this chapter will cover everything that you need to know. Let's start with the basics.

Just Setting It Aside – A Good Tactic to Begin With

Ideally, college planning should start the moment your child is born. This gives you enough time to develop a good plan and save enough money to make paying for education smooth. If you wait until your children are in high school, there's no way that you'll be able to save up hundreds of thousands in time without making sacrifices.

In 18 years, you can build a very nice foundation for your child's college. When they're born, start by putting $100 or $200 aside every month. Of course, it's best to put in as much as possible, but a couple hundred should be enough at the beginning. Whenever you feel like you can increase that amount by $50 or $100 per month, make sure to do it.

After a while, there will be enough money to put into a brokerage account. You'll also likely earn more money with time, so you can start adding more to the account. And by the time your kids are ready for college, you'll save enough for one to four years without trouble.

Now, there are different strategies that you can use when planning for college. You can go with a 529 or educational IRA account. There are also many state-sponsored options at your disposal, so let's dig deeper into them.

529, IRA, and Other State-Sponsored Plans

IRA and 401k withdrawals are a common way to pay for your kids' education. So, if you still haven't started planning your retirement, here's another reason to start. Now, you can't just take the money out of your IRA as you wish. You have to meet the IRS' criteria and be careful about how you withdraw your money.

For example, there's a 10% penalty on early withdrawals, and it is also taxable income. This way, the IRS wants to make sure that people keep money in their account for retirement, so that they don't have to rely on social security. To avoid the penalty, you must withdraw the money while your student is in an eligible institution. You can't use the funds to pay off student debt, but you can offset the impact of the repayments while your child is in college. Also, you're still obligated to pay the income tax on the money that you withdraw.

As for 529s, these are tax-advantaged savings plans, also known as qualified tuition plans. There are two types that you can choose from – education savings plans and prepaid tuition plans. Each state offers at least one of these options, so you might want to get informed on the one that you can apply for.

Education savings plans let you open an account where you'll save for all college expenses. These include:

- Tuition
- Mandatory fees
- Room and board

Prepaid tuition plans, on the other hand, are a bit more restrictive. They allow you to buy credits or units at eligible colleges, but do not pay for room and board.

As long as 529 funds get used for educational purposes, they're not subject to income tax. This goes for both federal and state taxes in most cases. But if the funds go towards elementary or secondary school tuition, some or all of it could be taxed, with a 10% penalty. This is something that you should keep in mind if you start planning while your kids are young, as you should.

What Are UGMA or Custodian Accounts?

UGMA (Uniform Gift to Minors Act) and UTMA (Uniform Transfer to Minors Act) accounts are basically custodian accounts. As such, they allow you to hold your child's assets until the age of majority.

UGMA accounts allow mutual fund, stock, and bond investments. On the other hand, you should not use them for high-risk assets like stock options. The majority of people use UGMA accounts to start adding cash to them over time. You can open the account under your child's name and SSN, after which you can start putting money into it.

Now, the greatest advantage of UGMA accounts is tax benefits. Every year, the first $1,100 of earning won't be taxable. The next $1,100 will get taxed at your child's bracket (usually very low). This is 10% in federal income tax. Everything above this amount will get taxed at the parent's bracket, up to 37% federal tax.

Now, to get the UGMA account to the point at which it's subject to taxation, you'll first have to put quite some money into it. For example, if you're earning 10%, it will take you $11,000 to earn $1,100 per year. If you're at 5%, you'll need $22,000. This is why it's so important to open that account on time and start filling it while your kids are still young.

Now, the disadvantage of UGMA accounts is that you have an obligation to give your child control over the assets when they reach the age of majority. Some children won't be responsible enough to actually use that money for college. Because of this, you must educate your children on this kind of responsibility. By the time they're ready for college, your children should be able to manage their UGMA funds wisely with your guidance.

Pay for All of It Out-of-Pocket vs. Education Loans

So far, we've covered some of the best strategies for college planning. As you now know, there are many options out there, so you can get ready for your child's education rather easily. Plus, it is manageable if you prepare over time. Even if you don't save for the entire four years, you can make a good start on it.

But what if it's too late for this? What if you're in the same situation as Mr. and Mrs. Jones who came to us because they hadn't saved anything?

Well, you'll have two options at your disposal. You can either pay for your children's education out-of-pocket or apply for student loans.

The Big Debate

There's really no right or wrong answer as to who should pay for your child's education. Every family is different, so you need to assess your financial situation and values.

Some parents decide not to pay so that they can teach their kids responsibility and hard work. If your child takes out a student loan, they'll tie themselves to work in order to repay the loan. Others don't want their children to go through this, so they'll help them out. For this reason, you should sit down with your family and decide on the best option that reflects your values.

If you decide to pay, we always suggest that you do it out of your bank account before you apply for the loan. Pay as much as you can out of your pocket, and then try to get a loan to help your child. You'll be able to repay that loan for up to 10 years, so you can come up with a plan for doing so as comfortably as possible.

You know your financial standing and your children better than anyone. Because of this, you should use your own judgment to see how you'll pay for their education. There are many grants and loans that can help you out, so do your research and come up with the best solution.

Paying Your Children to Help Your Business (and Help Pay for College)

If you own a business, you can help your child earn money for college by working for you. These days, children are getting more adept with technology from an early age. And as many businesses are largely driven by technology, you can help your children put those skills to good use.

If they decide to help you out, you can give them a small salary of $500-$1,000 per month. You can give it to them on a W-2 and put that money straight into the savings account.

In this case, you're getting deductions at your own rate. For example, if you're in the 35% bracket, and your child makes $10,000 per year from you, that's $3,500 in savings. If you're a sole proprietor, you won't have to pay any social security or Medicare tax until your children are 18. As a result, you'll have no costs aside from the forms.

If you own a corporation, you'll have to pay only the social security and Medicare tax, which will cost you a bit higher than 15%. Still, you'd save almost 20% that you'd have to pay in your own bracket. Add this up for

8-10 years of your child's earning power, and it will amount to quite some money. It will certainly cover the costs of putting away money for college.

The best thing that you can do is to put this college money into your children's UGMA or UTMA account. If you decide to go with the 529 or IRA, you'll want them to gift the money back to you, and then you'll put it into their account after they've earned the money.

So far, many of Bernstein Financial's clients have used this strategy to support their children's education. And they've had great experiences with it. If you're a business owner, this might be the best way to go about college planning.

Saving for Education

As you saw here, there are many ways to ensure that your children's education isn't a financial burden. This further proves the power of having a good plan in place. If you start while your children are still young, you can buffer one of the highest expenses that you'll encounter in your life.

So, if you haven't already, go ahead and explore the options outlined here. Think about the long run, and find a solution that will let you save the most money.

Of course, this doesn't mean that you don't have any options if you missed your chance to plan ahead. If you understand your cash flow and abilities, you can come up with a way to get your children through college smoothly. Many types of financial aid are available to you and your children, so it all boils down to finding the right one.

But what happens once your children's college funds are safe and secure? Well, it's time to get more serious about your retirement plans.

CHAPTER FOUR

How to Retire in Style – The Blueprint for Retirement Planning

In the previous chapter, you saw how Jeff and Mariam rectified the mistake of not planning for their children's college on time. When they came to Bernstein Financial, the couple finally understood what good planning is all about.

After they made the college plan, Jeff and Mariam decided to never underestimate the power of planning again. Because of this, they started working with us on their retirement plan.

First I gave them some courage pills from the jar on my desk (really M&M's), and told them to look at the snowboard next to me on the wall. I said, "when we plan properly we get to do the things we enjoy". I gave them some fidget toys to lessen the stress and we made sure the kids were happy playing Guitar Hero in the waiting room, then we were ready to begin.

Their goal was to have $1.5 million in their retirement account. At 5%, they'd earn $75,000 per year, or about $6,000 per month. They'd supplement this with social security and a couple of other investments, ending up with a total of around $90,000 per year.

Another important idea that we helped Jeff and Mariam with was to create different accounts for various purposes. They created a marriage account for their kids. This way, when the kids decide to get married, their parents wouldn't have to give them $30,000-$40,000 at once. They also created accounts for their kids and future grandkids so that they could buy them different things without hurting their cash.

These accounts ensured that Jeff and Mariam didn't have to take funds out of their retirement account until they actually retired. They covered all the relevant future expenses, protecting both their family and retirement.

This is a perfect example of retirement planning done right. They asked all the right questions that everyone planning for the future should consider.

Most importantly, they knew what their goals were. This is critical as every person sees an ideal retirement in a different way. Your goals determine the amount that you need as well as how you'll save for it.

Maybe you plan on downsizing to a smaller home in a quieter area. Maybe you want a beach house where you can enjoy your golden years to the fullest. You may want to travel, focus on your hobbies, or do all sorts of other things.

And all of those things will cost you. This is why you must know exactly how you want to spend your retirement, and how much money it will take to achieve your goals.

The last thing you want is to spend your retirement barely getting by and staying home all the time. After decades of hard work, you deserve to live an enjoyable and exciting life as a senior. So, let's dive into the things that you should consider to make this happen.

Pre-tax Pension Plans (401K, Uni-K, Profit Sharing, SEP, SIMPLE, Defined Benefit)

Similar to college planning, retirement planning offers a variety of strategies to use. Another similarity is that you should start setting money aside as early in life as possible. If you wait until you're 60, there's little chance that you won't be able to retire as comfortably as you should.

There are many types of pre-tax pension plans that can help you retire in style. These include:

- 401(k)
- Uni-K
- IRA
- Self-Employer Pension Plan
- SIMPLE plan
- Defined benefit plans

All of these plans allow you to deduct taxes while investing the money. For example, if you put $20,000 into your account, and you're in the 30% bracket, you can defer $6,000 in taxes.

It's important to mention that these accounts allow you to defer taxes, not save them. You'll take the money out at some point, and you'll have to pay taxes when you do. Still, there's a massive benefit to deferring your taxes this way. As you'll have to pay taxes much later, the money can sit in your account for a long time. As a result, you can earn the interest that compounds on the government's tax money.

There's also a type of account where there are no deductions. These include the Roth IRA and Non-Deductible IRA. The Roth IRA is a much better option as you don't have to pay any taxes on earnings if you leave the money in your account until you're old enough to use it. If you withdraw the funds earlier, you won't be able to reap this benefit.

How Much Do You Need?

How much money do you need to set aside to retire comfortably? Obviously, this is entirely up to you and your desired lifestyle. Figure out the amount of money that you want to have when you retire, and then work backward to see how much you should start investing.

For a simple example, if you need $2 million, divide this by the number of years you have until retirement. Then, divide this number by 12, and you'll see how much you should start setting aside. This will actually provide more than $2 million because of the earnings over 20 years which adds to your principal contributions.

How much will $2 million yield at retirement? If we take 5% as the standard, those $2 million will yield $100,000 per year, a little above $8,000 per month before taxes. Do not let the $2 million figure scare you, do the best you can, and it will add up nicely.

Of course, you may have other retirement plans or investments aside from the main one. So, put all those numbers together, and then figure out how much you need to start saving.

The Benefits of Creating Alternate Revenue Streams

Many of Bernstein Financial's clients go beyond retirement accounts. They're serious about investing in their future, which is why they create auxiliary income streams.

For example, some people decide to put a little less money into their pension and invest in real estate or after-tax brokerage accounts. Others invest in a side business or a piece of land that might grow in value with time.

We strongly advise that you adopt the same approach to retirement planning. If you do, you'll plant the seeds for a more stable and financially-free future. There are many smart investments that you can consider, so it would be a good idea to start supplementing your income with them.

Now, bear in mind that you should never do this instead of regular pension planning but alongside it. Why?

It's simple – every investment carries a certain degree of risk. And you surely don't want to gamble with your retirement. Regular retirement planning should be your safe haven to ensure a comfortable life no matter what happens. More risky investments should only be considered in addition to your planned retirement investment.

Because of this, you should spread your retirement efforts across different strategies. Think of it as a pie chart that you'll divide into a few pieces.

For example, your Roth IRA can be the biggest piece. Others can be real estate, brokerage accounts, and so on. The point is that you should try not to rely on a single source of income. It's the classic "don't put all your eggs in one basket" scenario. You want a diversified source of income that will fuel your desired lifestyle in your golden years.

And finally, you should have some conservative, along with some more liberal, investments. When you're younger, you can go with higher-risk investments. But as you get older, play it as safe as you can to ensure stability in the long run.

Constant Monthly/Quarterly/Yearly Investments

One of the biggest misconceptions that people have about retirement planning is that you need a very large amount of money to put in. But that isn't the case. Some of our most successful clients are building their future by setting aside a little at a time and leveraging the compounding effect.

Don't wait until you have a lump sum to invest in your retirement. By doing so, you'd lose quite a sum of money that your accounts could've built up. A much better alternative is to put in as much as you can every month, and then watch your equity grow.

While our clients keep investing and upping their money consistently, it doesn't mean that they make sacrifices. They still take vacations to desired destinations and buy the things they want. But they always pay themselves first by investing in their retirement. And if you do the same, you will see results.

Also, make sure to keep close track of your equity. Every once in a while, take a piece of paper or an Excel spreadsheet and itemize your assets and liabilities. Your equity should keep growing consistently, and you should see improvements every couple of years. If this doesn't happen, it means that you need to take some corrective action.

Retirement Savings Plan (sample)
John and Sally Jones (Ages 34 and 33)
Plan to retire at ages 66 and 65

	Current	Plus 1 year	Plus 5 year	Plus 10 year	Plus 20 year	Retirement Year Plus 32 year
401K John	$ 40,000	$ 46,000	$ 81,000	$ 140,000	$ 250,000	$ 450,000
401K Sally	$ 30,000	$ 35,000	$ 60,000	$ 120,000	$ 200,000	$ 320,000
After tax Investment	$ 10,000	$ 13,500	$ 40,000	$ 70,000	$ 140,000	$ 250,000
Home	$ 350,000	$ 360,500	$ 405,746	$ 440,000	$ 550,000	$ 750,000
Total	$ 430,000	$ 455,000	$ 586,746	$ 770,000	$ 1,140,000	$ 1,770,000

	Assets	Yearly Earnings	Monthly Earnings
401K John	$ 450,000	$ 22,500	$ 1,875
401K Sally	$ 320,000	$ 16,000	$ 1,333
After tax Investment	$ 250,000	$ 12,500	$ 1,042
Cash from Home	$ 350,000	$ 17,500	$ 1,458
Social Security Benefits-John		$	3,500
Social Security Benefits-Sally		$	2,500
Total Income to retire		$ 68,500	$ 11,708
Income tax		$ (6,850)	$ (1,171)
Net Cash to Retire		$ 61,650	$ 10,538

The above figures assume:
Consistent and slightly increasing investment in the 401K's and the After Tax Investment Account.
Selling the family home at retirement ($750K), buying a less costly home ($400K), and investing the balance.
Approximately 3% increase per year in the home value, and 5% increase in the pre and post investment accounts.
There are many ways to get to an adequate retirement income, this is just one example.

When Is It Too Late to Start, and What Happens if College Takes up All Retirement Income?

As we explained, you should start planning your retirement as early in life as possible. This way, you'll have enough time to create a diversified fund that will help you achieve your retirement goals.

But does this mean that it's too late to start if you're in your forties or fifties?

Not at all!

Sure, it might be too late if you're 65. But even when you're middle-aged, there's still a lot that you can do to create and execute a sound retirement plan. Some of our clients started when they were 40-45, and they've had excellent results. And the main reason for this is that they got serious about it.

Yes, you might be at a disadvantage if you start a bit later in life. You might not be able to get that $2 million goal. But you could save $1 million. And isn't that better than just squandering your money and having nothing at all?

The point is, as long as you keep moving from the starting point, your retirement will be that much more comfortable. While you might not achieve all your goals, you'll still go a long way towards your ideal lifestyle. The more committed you are to your plan, the more you'll be able to achieve your goals.

Also, you might feel compelled to tap into your retirement account to pay for your child's college education. We strongly advise against this, as it can put a massive dent in your fund and make it very hard to reach your goals.

If you can't afford college, try taking out a loan or telling your child to apply for one. Try to find a way through without sacrificing your future. As you saw in the previous chapter, there are many strategies for college planning. Explore your options, and be sure not to hurt your retirement.

Estimating Your Revenue and Cash Flow Needs at Retirement

There's no exact answer as to how much you need to retire comfortably. You know your current lifestyle and abilities the best, and the same goes for your ideal retirement. For this reason, you must take a close look at the future and see what would make your retirement enjoyable.

When you do, you'll have to figure out how much that will cost you. This might be tough as you can't predict every single expense that you might incur. This is one of the main reasons why insurance planning is so important. But aside from it, you'll still have to crunch some numbers to arrive at an accurate estimate.

The most common estimate that experts will advise you on will be approximately 75-80% of your pre-retirement income. While this is a decent point of reference, the actual amount can vary greatly.

Research shows that high-income, high-saving households need as little as 60% of their pre-retirement income. In some cases, the number can be even lower. At the same time, low-income, low-saving households might need almost 90%.

The thing is, many factors determine how much you'll need in retirement. This is why you should never try to make any estimates on your own. Rather, you should sit down with your tax professional or financial professional. They'll get a deep understanding of your situation and goals, after which they'll help you make all the necessary estimates.

The reason this is so important is that people often focus too much on their income or revenue when planning for retirement. They get bogged down in the details around how much they'll make. When, in fact, you should also estimate anticipated expenses.

You need to project all your future expenses and see what they amount to on a monthly basis. There are all sorts of charts that an expert can provide to help you with this.

Of course, you'll then estimate your future earnings based on what you can start setting aside. You can see if your fund will be able to generate the kind of income that will allow you to cover all expenses comfortably.

Yes, this is a process that requires a lot of work and thinking. It's vital that you go through it. Otherwise, how can you know if your retirement fund is moving in the right direction? Put all the relevant numbers in a spreadsheet, do some calculations, and you'll know exactly where you stand.

Adjusting Assets and Expectations to Meet Retirement Needs

Many times, clients will come to Bernstein Financial because they're afraid that they can't retire. They might already be in their sixties with too many expenses to stop working.

For example, you might still have a mortgage to take care of. Your monthly repayments might be quite high, so you'll have to work for an additional few years to bring the mortgage down as much as you can.

Or you can get creative and find a way to retire anyway.

Here's the thing . . .

There's almost always a solution to your retirement issues. You just need to know where to look for one.

In the above example, you could downsize to a smaller house in the suburbs. You could even move to a different city or state that has lower taxes. If you did so, your expenses would be drastically lower in an instant. You could use the money from the previous house to invest in an asset and create a stable stream of income to supplement your retirement. So, not only would you start saving more, but you'd have more money to spend on top of it.

This is only one of the many ways in which you can re-adjust your expectations to achieve your retirement goals. If you don't want to move away from your city, you can find different ways of boosting your cash flow.

Maybe you have high-interest debt like a credit card. Get serious and strategically pay it off, you'd automatically improve your bottom line. You could then work towards paying off other debts or trying to secure some passive income.

If your retirement plan doesn't work for any reason, there's a simple fix – revisit and update it. If you think outside the box, you can find a way to deal with just about any issue.

Retire Pockets Full of Cash

When people think about retirement, the first thing that comes to mind is often a 401(k) plan. In many cases, it's the only strategy that people can think of. But as you saw in this chapter, there are many other ways to plan for retirement and ensure that your golden years are fulfilling.

With so many options out there, it would be pretty crazy to retire empty-handed. Why would you live off of government handouts when you can create a plan that will provide you with the lifestyle that you deserve?

Remember, with any form of planning, you should start thinking about retirement as soon as possible. The sooner you trigger the compound effect, the more money you'll have in retirement. Besides, starting early allows you to experiment with different options until you eventually find the one that works best.

Unless you're almost about to retire, there's always time to start planning. And even if you are, you can always do something that will make your retirement income at least a bit more abundant.

Retirement planning is one of the smartest things that you'll ever do for yourself. Now, let's move onto something that you can do for others.

CHAPTER FIVE

Estate Planning – What You Can Do for Your Entire Family

There's a strong similarity between insurance planning and estate planning – most people don't want to think about either. They involve scenarios that people aren't comfortable discussing, which is why they don't even think about them. And this is a big mistake.

How so?

Here's a situation that perfectly explains the dangers of not having a clear estate plan.

Imagine a husband and wife who have two children. The couple owns some valuable assets, and everything is going well for the family. But then, the husband dies, and the wife inherits the assets.

Not long after, the wife remarries. She doesn't do any estate planning either. She dies, and all the assets go to her new spouse. The kids get left with nothing, there's resentment towards the new spouse, and the family falls apart.

Sadly, this isn't fiction for some families. You'd be very surprised by the number of people who've gone through a scenario similar to this one. And all because they were uncomfortable with estate planning.

It's vital to remove the idea that estate planning is tedious or painful, and it doesn't mean that you don't trust your spouse – it means that you don't want to leave your estate plan to chance. And you shouldn't. You never know what can happen in the future, so you need to do everything in your power to protect yourself and your loved ones.

Estate planning is one of the most effective ways to do this. And even though we're not lawyers, we strive towards helping our clients create a bulletproof plan. By doing so, we can guide them towards a more stress-free future.

And make no mistake – a lack of estate planning can bring about tons of stress that you don't want your family to go through. If you need proof, the next section will provide it.

If You Don't Have a Plan, Your State Has One for You – Probate

Let's look at another hypothetical example that explains what happens without estate planning in greater detail (please consult an attorney for proper advisement regarding matters relating to this entire chapter).

What would happen if, at one point in your life, you become incapacitated? You might be on life support without a way to discuss your options. Instead, your family has to make them for you. They have to decide whether they'll keep you on life support or pull the plug.

You probably think that I am being callous talking about death this way. Remember, try to get past the strong emotions and let's talk about the facts and finances.

You have no durable power of attorney, no living will, no trust, or regular will. In one word, you don't have the so-called trust package. And if there's no trust in force, the state takes over through probate.

Let's say that your parents want to keep you on life support, but your wife doesn't. What do you think happens then?

Well, they all go to court and have to endure an excruciating process that can take up to a year or more to complete. You'd expose your whole family to insane amounts of stress and worry. And your future will be decided by the person that comes out victorious. As long as they make a legal decision, it will be carried out.

Another common scenario is when a person has to go to a nursing home due to incapacity. Without a trust, the state will decide where you'd go in this case. And again, it could take them a long time to figure this out. You'd spend all this time not getting the care you needed.

All of the above can be easily avoided with some careful estate planning. You can name a person who'd manage all your funds in case you die or become incapacitated. At the same time, that person would have the power to make decisions and act in your best interest. No court, no struggle, no waste of money and time.

A similar scenario applies to your business. If something happens to you, you need a clear contingency plan in place. And you can make one through a cross-purchase agreement. It allows other partners in your business to buy shares or interest in case you retire, die, or become incapacitated. Without such an agreement in place, your business' continuity would be exposed to large risk.

To sum up, estate planning protects everyone around you. It helps you devise a plan for even the worst scenarios. This way, your loved ones wouldn't have to suffer more than they would if something bad happened to you. So, let's explore your estate planning options in more detail.

Living Trusts (Single, Joint, Separate, AB Trusts, QTIP Trusts)

Even if you don't have a trust, your funds would probably go to your spouse if something unfortunate happened. As mentioned, they'd have to go through probate, which would be a tedious process that would take months to complete.

What would your spouse do in the meantime? How would they get by until they receive the funds?

But that's not even the worst-case scenario. What if you had children, and both of you died or ended up incapacitated?

In the case of death, the state would give all the funds to your children at once. And this definitely isn't the best way to funnel the money to kids and young adults.

With a trust package, you can set up a payment dynamic that your children receive the money in an appropriate way. The amount will depend on their health, education, and other needs. You can rest assured that your children will have everything that they need without carelessly burning through the funds.

In case your estate is large, you can arrange an AB trust and split your trust into two pieces. This would double the tax exemption upon death. And as of 2020, the exemption is $11.58 million.

Resolving Complex Matters

A trust doesn't only ensure that your funds get distributed properly. It also ensures that they go to the right beneficiaries. And this can be extremely important in many cases.

The perfect example of this is blended families. Let's say that you're currently in your second marriage. You have two children from the first one, and your spouse does as well. You don't think that there's any need for planning as there are no issues between you. But then, something tragic happens to you, and all your funds go to your spouse.

What would happen if your spouse didn't like your children? It's simple – they'd get nothing. The spouse would take everything and give it to their own kids.

With an AB trust, you can help ensure that this doesn't happen. You can let your spouse distribute funds in the way you set out until the surviving spouse dies. Then, your surviving spouse's estate would go to her children, and your estate would go to your children.

An alternative would be to give the funds to your kids outright, with only a portion left for your spouse. There are many ways in which you could handle this scenario, and all of them would favor those that you care about the most.

And finally, a trust helps to mitigate custody battles over your children in case anything happened to you and your spouse. You can name the person who'd take care of the children, and it would be difficult to challenge your decision in the vast majority of cases.

All of the above speaks volumes about the importance of setting up a trust. The sooner you do it, the sooner you'll be able to put your mind at ease.

Irrevocable Life Insurance and Other Irrevocable Trusts

We've talked about some of the worst scenarios that you can find yourself in. Somebody had to, as these are usually the things that people try to push out of their minds. Hopefully, you now understand why you shouldn't do it.

But now, let's imagine a brighter scenario to balance things out a bit. Imagine that you owned a massive asset, say, a $30 million business. And while the business is going strong, there's not that much cash in it. Should anything happen to you, your heir might have to sell the business to pay for estate tax and other obligations.

Luckily, there's a very simple way around this – irrevocable life insurance trust.

An irrevocable life insurance trust protects your assets from estate tax or debt tax. The insurance covers all taxes, thereby allowing your heir to keep enjoying the income that it produces. At the same time, the insurance won't add to the estate tax that's due.

So, how does this work?

The grantor (owner of the business) places the asset in an irrevocable trust. From this point on, the grantor can't revoke or change any of the terms of the trust. The trustee and beneficiary provide consent for setting the terms and rules, and nobody can tweak or modify them.

This way, both the grantor and beneficiary get protection from the seizure of assets placed in the trust. You can avoid probate and reduce taxes, which are the main reasons why people go with irrevocable trusts.

This type of trust has a wide variety of applications, including:

- Taking advantage of estate tax exemptions. Assets in an irrevocable trust don't add to the estate's value. Therefore, the tax liability can be much lower.
- Preventing beneficiaries from mishandling or misusing the assets
- Gifting assets within the estate while still retaining their income
- Gifting the principal residence to heirs under looser tax rules

- Depleting a property for the sake of qualifying for government benefits

Now, irrevocable trusts are complex legal matters. They also involve fees that can be quite costly. For that reason, this option is primarily geared towards high-net-worth individuals.

If you're among them, or you'll become one at some point, you should definitely consider this kind of trust. It can have a great positive effect on your estate and give beneficiaries all the protection that they need.

Gifting, Charitable Remainder Trusts, and Charitable Giving Techniques

Another form of estate planning that you'll want to think about is gifting. For example, you can gift 3% of your assets to someone, after which the asset's value would get discounted upon your death.

This is because there would be multiple owners, and there's always a discount in value to encourage the owners to sell their portion. As a result, the beneficiary would enjoy tax exclusion.

This technique is commonly used for businesses. But you can apply a similar one to a property through charitable remainder trusts. If you had a property that you were renting out, you'd get the income from it while you're alive. Upon your death, a portion of the property would go to charity, thereby reducing the value of your estate. Plus, you'd get an upfront deduction for your contribution to a charitable trust.

Another technique that you can employ is to open a donor-advised fund (DAF). DAFs are very popular in estate planning, largely due to their simplicity. They're also suitable if you haven't dedicated a dollar amount to a certain charity, or you want to donate to multiple charities.

The way DAFs work is very straightforward. You open the account and make an initial contribution. The donation can be in the form of stock, cash, mutual fund, etc. You invest these assets in a DAF pre-approved investment option. You'd get an immediate deduction, even if the charitable grant request gets delayed until future years.

When you want to distribute your money, you call your DAF sponsor and file a grant request. You can file multiple requests if you want to support various charities.

All of the above options are an effective way to save taxes and protect your heirs and beneficiaries. And there are many more ways to make this happen. You should work with a professional to determine the option that would suit your needs the best.

There's one more technique that's worth mentioning here – cross-purchase agreements. We already discussed them, so let's explain how they work based on a real-life example.

Let's say that you and your business partner had a business worth $3 million. Both of you have families and own an equal amount of $1.5 million each. You can get life insurance for $1.5 million each with the other owner named as beneficiary.

If you died or became incapacitated, the other owner would receive $2.5 million. They'd use this money to purchase the stock from your spouse and become a sole owner. Your spouse would get the funds, and your business will be able to continue without interruptions.

Become the Protector of Your Estate

Hopefully, you now understand the vital importance of estate planning. It protects those around you from the consequences of unpredictable tragedies. The last thing you want is to make an unfortunate event even harder for your loved ones.

Because of this, you should explore the options outlined in this chapter. Depending on your situation, there will always be a few strategies that you can (and should) put in place. Creating a solid trust package will save your family a lot of time and money, and protect them from unnecessary stress.

Don't let your state take care of your assets and make important decisions for you. Not only is this a dreadful process, but there's a high chance that the state won't act as you would have planned. So, start planning your estate now, and provide those around you with the protection and control that they need.

Also, careful estate planning can do wonders for saving taxes. As you saw in the previous sections, there's a lot that you can do to minimize your assets' tax liability.

Of course, you should do everything in your power to bring your taxes to the absolute minimum. And the next chapter will explore more options for doing so.

CHAPTER SIX

It's Time to Save Some Money on Taxes – Tax Planning 101

When Greg first came to Bernstein Financial, his finances were quite messy. He complained about barely being able to break even each year despite a high income.

He also had issues related to his spouse Shannon's tendency for overspending. Shannon was self-employed, and her earnings were quite good. However, the expenses were too high to ensure a strong positive cash flow.

Greg liked his job, but he always felt like he wasn't making enough money. When, in fact, it was the couple's taxes that put a strain on their cash flow.

The first thing that we discovered was that Greg and Shannon weren't keeping close track of their expenses. After we itemized all costs, Greg realized that many of the expenses were not listed. Because of this, the couple didn't have a strong grasp on their finances.

After we analyzed their cash flow thoroughly, it was time to start focusing on taxes. And the key thing that we focused on was the contribution of their children to Shannon's business.

The couple got their kids to help with the business more. In return, they'd get $500 per month. With 75% of it going towards college planning, the rest would be a small allowance.

The main benefit of this was tax deductions. Both kids were under 18, which meant that Shannon didn't have to pay any taxes on the first $12,000 (for each child) that went into the college account. Kids started feeling better for helping Shannon's business, and the couple saved on taxes.

We covered a few other items, such as the home office and technology expenses. After lowering the taxes, Greg and Shannon had more cash flow to work with. We shifted our focus towards cash flow planning, and the couple was able to manage their money much more wisely. Instead of barely breaking even, they'd have some cash left at the end of each year.

A handful of minor adjustments made a world of difference to their cash flow and lifestyle. Let's see how proper tax planning can do the same for you.

Balancing Income Between Business and Personal Tax Returns

You should always strive towards keeping your taxes in the lowest legal range. Luckily, there are many ways to do this. And the most common methods are the deferral of taxes and saving of taxes.

An example of tax deferrals is when you place money in a pension fund and put off the taxes for when you withdraw the money in retirement. And when it comes to tax savings, there are all sorts of strategies that you can put in place to maximize your deductions.

This is especially true if you're a business owner. Depending on your business entity, there are different actions that you can take to bring your taxes to a minimum.

Both an LLC and S-Corp protect your personal assets from any business losses. Obviously, this also implies that you need to manage your personal and business funds separately. From the tax perspective, we call this "balancing the income and expenses between your business and personal returns". You need to find the best allocation of income to pass on to each shareholder or member.

To do this, it's best to prepare your individual and corporate or LLC return at the same time. It allows you to get a clear overview of your income and find the optimal distribution. You need to take maximum deductions of expenses, as well as different types of reimbursements to owner-employees. Your entity can benefit from many deductions, so make sure to explore them in full.

Deferral of Taxes vs. Saving Taxes

Deferring and saving taxes involve an entirely different set of strategies. While both options can benefit you, you should be careful when choosing your preferred one. You must assess your current position and determine the best way to keep your taxes at a minimum.

For example, people in high tax brackets can benefit greatly from tax-exempt accounts. This is because their tax bracket is very high. These accounts traditionally have less earnings, but the tax-exempt status can make them equivalent to a much higher return.

You can open a tax-exempt account and invest in assets such as bonds. As your account grows, you can access the income tax-free. When you retire, you can draw the funds, but you may have (hopefully) some capital gains.

As far as tax deferral goes, a 401(k) and traditional IRAs are among the most common options. And the way these accounts work is rather simple.

Let's say that you had a taxable income of $50,000. If you decide to put $5,000 into the retirement account, you only pay tax on $45,000. When you retire, any withdrawals will be taxable. However, you'll likely be in the lower bracket when you retire. Regardless of your tax rates, you'll be earning money on the government's deferred taxes.

Plus, by deferring taxes, you get to grow your fund much sooner. You can earn interest and dividends on those deferred taxes, meaning that your fund can compound more effectively.

Ideally, you'd strike a balance between after-tax saving and tax deferrals programs. And this is why planning is so important. If you're smart with the numbers, you can save money right now and in the future.

Equity Investments vs. Income-Earning Investments

Investing in assets that spin off income seems like an obvious thing to do. You want your investment to start paying off as quickly as possible and give your income a boost. But from the tax perspective, this may not be the best idea.

The reason for this is clear enough. The more income your assets generate, the higher your taxes. And the higher your bracket, the more money you'll lose to taxes. If you're already making a lot of money, adding to your cash flow might not be the best idea tax-wise. Instead, you might want to adopt a long-term mindset.

In other words, you'll want to invest in an asset that builds up equity over time. It should be an asset that doesn't turn around a lot of cash in your high bracket while still growing in value.

Yes, this added value will be subject to capital gains taxes. But you can defer these taxes, as we discussed in the previous section.

For example, you can buy a property with a high depreciation that's still increasing in value. You won't have to pay high taxes, and you'll still have a valuable asset. When you retire, or the depreciation runs out, you can sell the asset and cash in on your investment.

Of course, this isn't a scenario that applies to everyone in the same way. It all boils down to your income and tax bracket. So, if you're a high-income, high tax-bracket person, equity investments can be an excellent idea.

Is Paying a Lot of Taxes Bad?

It goes without saying that people don't like taxes very much. You'll be out of pocket while stressing about all sorts of regulations. But does this mean that paying high taxes is a bad thing?

Actually, it doesn't!

How so?

Think about it. . . .

If you're paying a lot of taxes, it means that you're making a lot of money. If you're an NBA player making $10 million a year, your taxes will be very high. But at the same time, you have the kind of money that most people can only dream of.

And if you don't pay much in tax, it usually means that there's not that much income to tax in the first place. Your income might be small, and that's far worse than having to pay taxes. You might be an investor who keeps making poor decisions that don't generate income.

Now, it's reasonable to think that this is a bit contradictory. After all, this entire chapter is about minimizing your taxes.

You must understand the difference between paying a lot of taxes and wasting money. While the former isn't bad, throwing your money away on taxes that you can legally avoid definitely is. This is especially true when there are so many ways to bring your taxes to a minimum. With careful planning, you'll never have to pour money down the drain.

Paying Your Children to Help with the Business

We already discussed the value of letting your children help your business from the college planning perspective. We also explained how this could help you save money on taxes.

Now let's talk a bit more about how to reap these benefits. There are a few rules that you need to follow if you want to hire your child in a way that will maximize the tax savings legally and without hassle.

First of all, your child must be an actual employee (team member) of the company. In other words, they must do a job that directly contributes to your operations. It doesn't have to be an indispensable service, but it must be business-appropriate. Things like mowing the lawn or babysitting fall under personal services, so you won't be eligible for any tax deductions. By contrast, if your child does yard work on the business property, this would fall under a deductible rental business expense; as would helping with technology be an ordinary business expense.

Next, you must go through the same legal process as if you were hiring someone from the outside. This means that you still need all the right paperwork, including:

- USCIS Form I-9
- IRS Form W-4
- Employment Eligibility Verification

And finally, your child's salary should be reasonable. You can't pay them $100 per hour for cleaning and expect tax deductions. While you should pay them as much as you can, it should still be within the range of what is reasonable wages for the work performed.

You must take into account the value of your child's services to the business. The safest thing to do is to see how much other companies are paying team members for similar services. Find the appropriate amount, and make sure that you actually pay them and file all of the appropriate government payroll tax forms.

You can deposit the money into your child's Roth IRA, 529, or other accounts that we discussed. Not only can you save a lot on taxes, but you can also teach your child about work ethic from a young age.

File Taxes on Time

Probably the best way to waste a lot of money is by not filing your taxes on time. People often complain about preparation fees or the money that they'd pay for an advisor. But at the same time, they'll easily pay thousands of dollars in penalties.

Don't let yourself get into this situation. It pays much more to prepare tax filings on time and avoid the hassle and stress of doing it last-minute. Plus, the consequences of not filing on time can be severe.

Obviously, the first thing that you'll face is penalties. If you don't file on time, you'll be subject to a penalty of up to 50% on your overdue tax. Plus, the IRS will charge you interest according to the federal short-term rate, which is usually between 3% and 6% annually.

Of course, you'll also go through the scary experience of getting notices from the IRS. If this has ever happened to you, you already know how much panic it can cause. Add this panic to lack of proper planning, and you'll make the problem much worse.

What do you think would happen to your refund if you fail to file on time? It's simple – you might lose it. The IRS won't issue you a refund if you haven't done your part of the job. They have the right to hold onto it, so you might never see your money depending on how late you file (ie: 3 years late).

Next, failing to pay the IRS is the same as defaulting on any other payments. As a result, it can put a stain on your credit report. You might not get the loans that you need, or the terms may be unfavorable.

This is only the tip of the iceberg when it comes to all the consequences of not filing and paying your taxes on time. And you can avoid them all by simply planning ahead of time. Stay on top of your tax filings and payments, and you'll avoid trouble with the IRS.

Maximize Pension Contributions

We already explained the importance of maximizing your pension contributions. This allows you to build your fund more quickly while deferring tax for later periods.

However, you'll also want to have an after-tax fund that you'll pull money from, especially when it comes to larger sums. Otherwise, you might end up like Joe, a client of ours. Joe came to us after setting aside nice sums of money as pre-tax contributions for many years. He'd built a $3 million fund by the time he retired.

He had very little money in his after-tax account, which ended up causing financial discomfort. Joe wanted to withdraw $50,000 to buy a new car, so he came to us for tax information. He wanted to know how much he'd need to draw to buy that car.

As all of the money was pre-tax, we told him that he needed $85,000 because of his tax bracket. Needless to say, Joe ended up regretting the fact that he hadn't built a solid after-tax fund to allow for a balance of distributions between pre- and post-tax accounts.

This is why we always advise our clients to focus on after-tax accounts also.. By doing so, you can have distributions that you can manage from your pre-tax and post-tax accounts more easily and with less stress.

Don't Miss a Chance to Save on Taxes

Having a firm grasp on your taxes is an effective way to save a lot of money in the long run. Better yet, there are many strategies that can make this happen. Browse the options outlined here and see which of them apply to your situation the best.

Also, don't neglect to file your taxes on time. There's too much hassle and waste involved if you don't, so try to make the IRS filings a priority. If you can't do it alone, it's much better to pay a professional than to face penalties and interest. An advisor can save you a lot of headaches and a lot of money, so you might want to consider going with one.

CHAPTER SEVEN

Start Planning Your Future

Now that you know what it takes to plan for a secure and financially-free future, it's time to start putting your knowledge to good use. Financial planning and life are not separate entities … it's about understanding options, taking baby steps in planning, long term planning, knowing that when we flounder, it's human …. we redefine our goals and move forward.

Go ahead and take a close look at your cash flow to determine your current standing. Remember to be honest with yourself instead of tweaking the numbers to your liking. You're already spending your money in a certain way, and putting it all on paper doesn't change anything. It only gives you a detailed overview of your finances so that you can start making smart decisions from a better perspective.

If you want to boost your cash flow, taxes will often be the first thing that you'll want to look at. In many cases, your taxes hide many opportunities to unlock more cash and boost your disposable income. You should also trim your unnecessary expenses as much as you can, or find a way to make more.

At this point, you'll be ready to do some planning. Make sure to have all the necessary types of insurance that will protect you from life's unpleasant surprises. You can neither see nor change the future, so protecting yourself is the only option that you have.

Speaking of the future, it's never too late to start preparing for retirement. The sooner you start, the more comfortable your lifestyle will be. Once you're sure that you can put your children through college smoothly, start investing in your own future.

And lastly, think about the impact that tragic events would have on those around you. If you haven't already, now would be the perfect time to start planning your estate. With a good plan in place, you can minimize the negative impact that death or incapacity can have on your loved ones.

We understand that this is a lot to cover. But nobody says that you have to do it all at once. In fact, you should take your time to do some research and find the best strategies. What matters is that you start as soon as you're ready. And there's no better time to start than right now.

MICHAEL BERNSTEIN

Michael Bernstein EA, MBA is a certified tax expert and CEO of Bernstein Financial Services, a consultancy firm that has catered to construction clients and small businesses for over 30 years. He is also the host of *Your Working Out Accountant* on YouTube. Follow Mike for more advice about personal and business finance on social media.

🖥 **socal.bernsteinfinancial.com**

in **linkedin.com/in/michael-bernstein-ea-mba**

▶ **https://rebrand.ly/sq9te**

Made in United States
Orlando, FL
23 February 2022

15091880R00051